W9-BHU-326

Light
vs.
Dark

by Clara MacCarald

The Child's World®
childsworld.com

Published by The Child's World®
1980 Lookout Drive • Mankato, MN 56003-1705
800-599-READ • www.childsworld.com

Photographs ©: Chayapat Karnnet/Shutterstock
Images, cover, 1; Shutterstock Images, 5, 6, 10,
13; Kevin Cass/Shutterstock Images, 9; Andrei
Bortnikau/Shutterstock Images, 15; iStockphoto,
16; Joy Brown/Shutterstock Images, 19;
Diyana Dimitrova/Shutterstock Images, 20

ISBN 9781503844469 (Reinforced Library Binding)
ISBN 9781503846616 (Portable Document Format)
ISBN 9781503847804 (Online Multi-user eBook)
LCCN 2019956649

Printed in the United States of America

About the Author

Clara MacCarald lives in a forest in New York with her family. She writes books for kids on subjects such as science and history. When not writing, she can be found holding woolly bear caterpillars with her daughter or herding toads off the driveway.

TABLE of CONTENTS

CHAPTER ONE

Light and Dark

Cora pulls the blankets up to her chin. Outside, lights shine down on the street. But her bedroom is dark.

Cora sneaks over to her dresser and grabs her flashlight. She turns the flashlight on. A circle of yellow hits the wall. She smiles as she makes the light dance. Wherever the light goes, the darkness goes away. She puts her hand in front of the flashlight. Her hand makes a shadow on the wall.

The door opens and light spills into the room. Cora looks up. Her dad stands in the doorway. He tells her it is time for bed. As she goes to sleep, Cora wonders: what are light and dark?

Flashlights are often used to create light in dark places.

Earth gets waves of light from the Sun.

Light acts like a wave of **energy**. Waves of light are the fastest things in the world. Light lets people see the world. Colors come from light. Plants, animals, and people can use light energy.

Darkness is what appears when there is no light. Darkness is not made of energy. There are no dark waves. Objects in the dark look black. People need light, but they also need darkness.

CHAPTER TWO

Waves on the Move

Light has to come from somewhere. Something makes light. A fire burns. A lamp turns on. Lightning strikes. Once light waves are made, they are always moving. Light waves move in straight lines until they hit something. When light waves bounce off something, people can see whatever the object is.

Nothing moves faster than light waves. Light can travel 186,000 miles (300,000 km) in a second. Light travels even faster than sound. When Grace sees lightning hit several miles away, the flash reaches her eyes almost instantly. The sound takes longer to travel to Grace's ears. She does not hear the thunder for several seconds.

People see lightning
before they hear thunder.

Shadows form when light cannot travel through an object.

Light

Darkness does not move on its own. Darkness appears when a light source stops making light. When objects block waves of light, shadows form. Shadows can move when the object making them is moved.

Not all objects make shadows. Some objects let light go all the way through. For example, light travels through the glass in a window.

Light can bend when it goes through something. Michael can see light bend in the bath when he puts his hand under the water. His arm looks like it is not straight anymore.

Mirrors have glass. But mirrors do not let light go through. A mirror is usually a piece of glass with a thin layer of metal on its back. The metal **reflects** light. A mirror reflects light so well that the mirror shows the scene in front of itself.

Mirrors reflect light to show images of the person or object in front of them.

13

CHAPTER THREE

Rainbows of Color

Without light, the world would be pretty dull. Colors appear because of light. Light waves have different sizes. Each wave size is a different color. Light waves can be red, orange, yellow, green, blue, indigo, and violet. Red waves are the longest. Violet waves are the shortest.

    We see color based on how light waves are **absorbed** or reflected by objects. Waves of many colors hit an object. Some waves bounce off the object. Other waves are absorbed by it. The color of the waves that bounce off are the color that the eye can see. Drew sees a red car drive by. Red waves bounce off the car. This creates the color Drew sees. The car absorbs all of the other light waves.

A car appears red because only red waves bounce off it.

Black objects absorb all light waves.

White light is special. White light contains all the other colors of light. White objects cause all light waves to bounce off. It is possible to separate the different colors within white light. Rainbows appear when water drops in the air bend white light from the sun. This reveals the separate colors. The colors appear as a **spectrum**. Water drops sprayed from a hose can also make rainbows. So can pieces of glass shaped like triangles, called **prisms**.

Black is another special color. Black objects absorb all light waves. A black truck drives past Drew. It is black because its paint absorbs all the light waves.

Drew's eyes see the truck as black. People also see black when there is no light. This is why objects that normally look colorful appear black in a dark place.

There are some colors that people cannot see at all. Many kinds of light are outside of the rainbow humans can see. One example is **ultraviolet light**. These waves are even smaller than violet waves. Bees and other bugs can see ultraviolet light. Some flowers have circles in the center that reflect ultraviolet light. The circles show bees where to go to get pollen.

CHAPTER FOUR

Light Power

Light is a form of energy. This means it can create heat. Sam feels the power of light on a sunny day. Standing in the bright light, she begins to sweat. She runs to the big tree in her yard. The dark shade blocks the light energy. Sam begins to feel cooler.

Light power can do more than make people feel hot. Plants use light to make food. Cells in plant leaves use light to do this. When the sun shines down, the materials absorb light. The leaves make food. Energy from the sun is stored in the food. The plant uses the power to live and grow.

Being in the shade is cooler than being in the sunlight.

People can use solar panels to turn sunlight into electricity.

Some animals eat plants to power themselves. Other animals eat the plant-eating animals. People eat plants and animals. All of that food has energy from the sun.

People can also use energy directly from the sun. People do not have leaves to catch light. Instead, people must use **solar panels**. Solar panels look dark because they take in most of the light that hits them. Solar panels turn light energy into **electricity.**

If it was always dark, people would have nothing to eat. People would also bump into everything. But if it was always light, people would have a harder time sleeping. And without shade, people would have no way to take a break from the sun on hot days. Both light and dark are needed for life.

Light vs. Dark

Light	Dark
Comes from a source	Appears where there is no light
Is a form of energy	Has no energy
Is a kind of wave	Is not a wave
Travels faster than anything else	Cannot move
Makes colors	Appears black

Glossary

absorbed (ab-SORBD) Something that is absorbed is taken inside something else. A black shirt absorbed all of the light waves.

electricity (i-lek-TRIS-i-tee) Electricity is a type of energy that can flow through wires. People use electricity to power computers.

energy (EN-ur-jee) Energy is a measure of something's ability to do work or create change. Animals eat food to gain energy.

prisms (PRIZ-uhmz) Prisms are clear, solid objects, often with a triangular base, that light can pass through. Prisms can create rainbows.

reflects (ri-FLEKTZ) Something that reflects throws back light or images. A mirror reflects people's faces.

solar panels (SOH-lur PAN-uhls) Solar panels are flat boards that catch energy from the sun. Some houses have solar panels on the roof.

spectrum (SPEK-truhm) A spectrum is bands of color lined up in a row. A rainbow is a spectrum.

ultraviolet light (uhl-truh-VYE-uh-lit LITE) Ultraviolet light is a kind of light people can't see. Some insects can see ultraviolet light.

To Learn More

In the Library

Crane, Cody. *Light*. New York, NY: Children's Press, 2019.

Fliess, Sue. *Flash and Gleam: Light in Our World*. Minneapolis, MN: Millbrook Press, 2020.

Wick, Walter. *A Ray of Light: A Book of Science and Wonder*. New York, NY: Scholastic Press, 2019.

On the Web

Visit our website for links about light and dark:

childsworld.com/links

Note to Parents, Teachers, and Librarians: We routinely verify our Web links to make sure they are safe and active sites. So encourage your readers to check them out!

Index